CHALKDUST

Prayers of Encouragement for Teachers

Elspeth Campbell Murphy

Originally published by Baker Book House.

Copyright © 1979, 2003, 2010 by Elspeth Campbell Murphy

ISBN: 978-1-5040-3024-3

Distributed in 2016 by Open Road Distribution
180 Maiden Lane
New York, NY 10038
www.openroadmedia.com

To my husband, Michael,
and to the children and staff of
Jonesville Elementary School
Yemassee, South Carolina
and of
Albert Einstein Elementary School
Hanover Park, Illinois

CONTENTS

Preface   13

Part 1: Prayers for the Children

For the Slow Learner   16

For the Child with Special Needs   17

For the Very Bright Child   18

For the Troubled Child   19

For the Child I Especially Like   20

For the Child I Don't Especially Like   20

For the Quiet Child   21

For the Class Clown   22

For the Rejected Child   23

For the Child Who Lies and Steals   25

For the Unmotivated Child   27

For the New Child   27

For the Child Whose Brother I Taught   28

7

CONTENTS

For the Latchkey Child   29

For the Child Who Adores Me   30

For the Child Who Doesn't Like Me   31

For the Chatterbox   32

For the Restless Child   33

For the Child Who Fights   34

Lament   35

For the Child from Another Language and Culture   36

For the Child Whose Family Is Going
    Through a Divorce   37

For the Abused Child   38

On the Forgiving Spirit of Children   39

Jesus and the Children   40

In Praise of Children   41

Part 2: Prayers Throughout the Year

At the Summer Workshop   44

At the Teacher's Supply Store   44

After Waking Up from a School Nightmare   45

In My Classroom the Week Before School Starts   46

On the Night Before School Starts   47

On the First Day of School   48

Before the Class Comes Marching In   49

This Kid Has a Bad Reputation   50

CONTENTS

On the Night of Open House   51

During the Excitement of Holidays   53

On the Night of the Big Program   54

When a Child Leaves in the Middle of the Year   55

When It Might Be a "Snow Day"   56

In the Middle of a Long, Dull Stretch   57

At Grading Time   58

When My Class Is the Pits   59

When a Child Is Going to Be Retained   60

The Child I Never Got to Know   61

On the Last Day of School   62

Part 3: Prayers for Special Times

Sunday Night Insomnia   66

On the Day of the Field Trip   67

When the Whole Class Flunks the Test   69

During the Fire Drill   70

When I Get Flak   72

At the End of a Good Day   74

On a Rainy Day   74

In the Middle of a Bad Day   76

When My Class Is the Greatest   77

On the Morning of the Standardized Test   77

At the Teachers' Workshop   78

CONTENTS

After Hearing That a Child's Parent Has Died   79

After Losing My Temper   80

When a Child Comes Back to Visit After
Many Years   81

Before Being Evaluated   83

After Being "Pink-Slipped"   84

After the Gripe Session   85

Part 4: Prayers for the Teacher

For the First-Year Teacher   88

For Renewal   92

For Help in Listening   93

For the "Why Am I Not Doing Anything
Important?" Blues   95

For Self-Acceptance   96

For Perspective   98

For Confidence   100

For Consistency   100

For the Substitute   101

When I'm the Teacher—Everywhere   103

For the Parent-Teacher Conference   103

For the Teacher Who's Going into Real Estate   104

For the Teacher Next Year   105

In Praise of Books   107

CONTENTS

In Praise of Learning   108

In Praise of a Teacher   109

On Showing Love   110

Part 5: Prayers for Parents and Other Grown-Ups

For the Parents of a Gifted Child   114

For the Parents of a Struggling Child   114

For the Parent of a Coddled Child   116

For the Troubled Parents   116

In Praise of Parents   117

For the Principal   118

For the Librarian   120

For the Consultants   120

For the Team   121

Schooldaze   123

At the School Board Meeting   123

PREFACE

I t is one of the paradoxes of teaching that, while there are cer-
tain experiences and feelings common to all of us, teachers
often feel so alone.

I think that's the reason *Chalkdust* has hit such a responsive
chord. One teacher after another has told me, "I read one medita-
tion and thought, 'Yes! That's just how it is! That's exactly what
it feels like!'"

This universality of what it means to be a teacher never ceases
to amaze and delight me. My own teaching experience has ranged
from an inner city of the industrial north, to the rural Gullah culture of coastal South Carolina, to a typical suburb west of Chicago.
Yet no matter where you teach or what grade, it all comes down to
this: you and your kids.

But did you ever get the feeling you're being watched? Education is much on the news these days, and it seems that almost everyone has something to say about it. Widespread interest in education is good, of course, but any discussion of education inevitably
comes back to the teacher. As a result, teachers are feeling scruti-
nized, even blamed. Teaching is hard enough without all of this
added pressure. So it is my hope that these prayers of encouragement will be just that: a source of encouragement—and even some
fun.

13

No one ever said teaching is easy (at least no one who has ever taught), but the influence on young lives is beyond measure. I learned recently that one of the most common reasons people hire private detectives is to find former teachers so that these grateful students can thank them. How about that?

Chicago
March 2003

PART 1

PRAYERS FOR
THE CHILDREN

Learning is a treasure that will follow its owner everywhere.

Chinese proverb

For the Slow Learner

Oh, Father,
this child is so slow,
and I am so impatient.
We are both trying hard,
and I desperately need to see some success.

If only I could see a little progress—
slow, plodding progress.
But the word he read yesterday
he can't read today.
The math concept he seemed to grasp yesterday
has slipped away today.

And somewhere inside me
discouragement is moaning, "Give up."

Help me not to listen.

Help me instead to listen for your voice
reminding me of all the good and true things
I've learned about teaching.

Remind me that progress is more a spiral staircase
than a straight flight of steps;
that learning rarely moves at a heartening pace;
that it is more likely to dip and double back,
and move on in little spurts of growth.
So help me, Father,
not to give up when we move so slowly,
or stand still,
or even seem to slip backward.

Give to me, and to this child,
the sure and steady faith to keep on trying.

But, Father, when I grit my teeth and try so hard
that I am overcome with impatience,
let me hear your still, small voice saying, "Relax!"

For the Child with Special Needs

Father, she's just like all the other kids.

Except that she has
the longest, reddest hair
in the whole class.

Except that she got
a real, live German shepherd puppy
for her birthday,
and no one else in the whole class
has a dog like that.

Except that she can
say all of "The Night Before Christmas"
whenever anybody asks her to,
without ever getting stuck.

Except that the afternoon sun
slanting in the window
glints on the metal brace
clamped around her leg.

Except for all that,
she's just like all the other kids.

17

For the Very Bright Child

Father,
I don't have to plead for her attention
or devise tricks to keep it.
She eagerly takes in everything I have to teach her,
and then goes off to learn more on her own.

I am delighted.

But I am also concerned,
for already I detect signs of arrogance in her.

Father,
with all her knowledge,
let her get understanding.
Keep her from assuming that intelligence
can take the place of compassion
or humor.

And as her teacher,
keep me from setting undue store by brilliance.
Let my classroom be both a relaxed
and an exciting place,
where each child—from the slowest learner to the gifted—
does the best he can,
where the challenge of learning
never overpowers the joy.

For the Troubled Child

Father,
I look into this little face that never smiles,
and I wonder what can be going on
behind those troubled eyes.

If I am impatient with her behavior,
it's because I don't understand it.
I'm bewildered.
And even a little frightened.
Oh, Father,
I fear that this world is a cold and hostile place
for some of these,
your children.
They seem preoccupied with troubles
they can't begin to understand.

As her teacher,
I feel at a loss to help this little girl.
I don't even know what's wrong.

Guide me, Father.
Show me my place in all of this.
Remind me daily
that this child is infinitely precious
in your sight.

And help this child
to believe that she matters to you
because I've been able to show her
that she matters to me.

For the Child I Especially Like

He walks in,
and the room brightens a little.
He carries an aura of well-being and happiness
wherever he goes.
He greets the world openly,
reaching out with acceptance and warmth.
What a joy it is to teach a child
who is so well-balanced and unselfconscious;
who's disciplined, but not compulsive;
high-spirited, but not rowdy;
intelligent, but not arrogant.
Guide me, Father,
as I try to guide this young person
to whom so much has been given.
And thank you, Father,
for granting me the pleasure of his company.

For the Child I Don't Especially Like

Help me, Father.
I don't like this kid.
And I confess I'm inclined to pick on him.
He has a peculiar knack
for being in the wrong place at the wrong time,
and often he bears the blame
when I am mad at the world.
I seem to be after him for every little thing,
but, Father,
there are *so many* little things.
A more annoying child would be very hard to find.
He gets on my nerves,

and when I'm nervous,
I take it out on him.
It's a vicious circle.

Father, help me as I grapple
with these feelings of irritation and dislike.
Help me, at least, to be fair.
And then perhaps
fairness can lead to kindness,
and kindness to affection.

For the Quiet Child

The day began with more than the usual commotion,
and it was mid-morning
before I realized she wasn't there.

Forgive me, Lord.

Make me sensitive to your quiet ones,
for in a loud and pushy world
they are so often overlooked.

Make me sensitive.
Their silence may be hiding inner turmoil,
so let me be quick to see in their faces
those things they cannot tell me in words.

Make me sensitive.
Keep me from thinking
that there is something innately wrong with silence,
that all children should be boisterously the same.
You have filled the world,

21

and my classroom,
with dazzling variety;
keep me from trying to homogenize it.

Help me to take notice of my shy students,
and to draw them out,
but without violating their freedom to be themselves.
Let me encourage them to stand up for their rights,
but keep me from violating their basic right to silence.

Lord, thank you for your quiet ones,
for in a loud and pushy world,
they are a calm oasis
and a balm for the soul.

For the Class Clown

There he goes—
an exuberant bundle of noise and laughter.
He doesn't walk, he bounces.
He doesn't talk, he whoops.
There he goes—
a little clown
dedicated to the proposition that life is hilarious.
His every action is an antic;
his every move, a slapstick pantomime.

Father, I confess that
his sparkle,
his zest,
his *joie de vivre*,
doesn't rub off—
it just rubs.

Five minutes in his presence,
and I'm reduced to an exhausted, shrieking old crone.

Oh, Father, give me a little more patience.
Soothe my frayed nerves,
and restore my good humor.
Let this child teach me
to take delight in life,
even as I teach him
to take delight in moderation.

For the Rejected Child

You see her, Lord Jesus,
standing all alone on the edge of the playground.
A forlorn and funny little figure,
whose clothes are not quite right,
whose hair is not quite right,
whose speech is not quite right.

You see her, Lord.
A funny little figure standing alone,
because in the grim opinion of all the other ducklings,
she's not quite right.

What am I to do?
I can't force the other children to play with her.
That would only make matters worse,
would only turn a spotlight
on her pain.

I look at her standing there,
blink hard,

and look away.
Oh, Lord Jesus,
why do there have to be outcasts?
If I were in charge,
there'd be none of that;
we'd all be emphatically
equal.
No one would be cast aside
to suffer the pangs of loneliness
because of funny clothes
and funny hair
and funny speech.
We'd all be, well—
acceptable ducklings.

But I hear your firm rebuke.
I want acceptable ducklings;
you want glorious swans.
Your ways are not my ways.
You see the infinite value
of the weak,
the humble,
and even the funny-looking.
And who knows but that the pain of being different
might be your preparation
for greatness?
So give me some of your vision.
Help me to see the promise
in that lonely little girl.
Show me where her talents lie,
so that I can show them to her.
Let me give to her—
herself.

Thank you for reminding me
that there is no one
more loving than you,
no one more sensitive to the abandoned
and the lonely than you.
You—
who flung wide your arms of love
and gathered in the outcasts:
the half-breeds,
the lepers,
the prostitutes,
the maimed.

Oh, Lord Jesus,
open your arms a little wider,
and gather in that forlorn and funny little figure—
and me.

For the Child Who Lies and Steals

Oh, Father,
here we go again.

Caught red-handed,
he looks at me out of solemn eyes
and swears he's not to blame.

"Look," I say,
hating the earnest pomposity of my voice,
"It's bad enough to steal something;
it only makes matters worse
to lie about it."
And the quizzical frown on his face

seems genuine:
if you're caught stealing,
what else would you do but lie?

But it's the lying
that really gets to me, Father.
Time and again
I have looked searchingly into his face,
unable to tell whether "lie" or "truth"
was written there.

Time and again
he has broken trust,
making a mockery
of the benefit of the doubt.

And time and again
I have been tempted
to shrug
and let him go.

But, Father,
how can I let him go?
How can I not tell him
that it is wrong to lie and cheat and steal?

He's a moral infant, Father,
and sometimes I feel as though I'm raising him alone.
Surely I can't be the only one
who loves him enough to tell him, "No."

Oh, Father,
if I'm not the one who can reach him,
please send him someone who can.

For the Unmotivated Child

Lord, I'm exasperated!
He won't even try.
Children with far less natural ability
struggle on like determined little tortoises—
while the hare just sits,
his mind asleep.

Lord, I've tried so hard to rouse him.
I've prodded and threatened and cajoled.
And if there's some incentive I've overlooked,
some method I haven't tried,
please show me what it is.

But perhaps the time for prodding has passed.
Perhaps the time for decision is here.
And it is a decision only he can make:
to wake himself up
and run the race that is set before him.

Please let him make that decision, Lord,
before it is too late,
and he is left far, far behind.

For the New Child

Oh, I know,
it's hard to be the new kid.
But, Father, really.
The room is far too crowded as it is!
Where will I put another child?
And coming so late in the year—

27

when we're all so far along in math—
how he'll catch up, I just don't know.
And the reading program he was in
was totally different from this one.
And all the plants for the science project are coming up,
and we'll have to start his from scratch, and . . .

Oh, Father,
there he stands
in the doorway,
with a brand-new red notebook
clutched at his side.

And the little hand
I hold in mine
when I introduce him to the class
is trembling.

He's not "another kid";
he's Tony.
"We're so glad to have you in our class, Tony,"
I hear myself saying.

And suddenly,
I mean it.

For the Child Whose Brother I Taught

Lord, I have to talk about this kid—
He's not at all what I expected.
His brother was a shining star,
Superkid, perfected.

28

His older brother took home A's.
He drops his C's in puddles.
His brother was precise, intense.
This kid's a cheerful muddle.
His brother always raised his hand,
Followed instructions To The Letter . . .
What's that, Lord?

You know,
You're right!
I *do* like this kid better.

For the Latchkey Child

Father,
with what a mixture of anxiety and pride
he shows me the house key
tied firmly to his belt.
Other children are old hands
at going home to an empty house.
But this is his first day,
his first day of being alone and nervous,
of hearing funny noises.
"You'll be fine," I say.
"What rules did your mother give you?"
He has them all down pat.
 Lock the door after me.
 Phone Mom as soon as I get in.
 Don't tell any callers I'm home alone.
 Don't open the door to strangers.
 Take the meat out of the freezer.
 Set the table.
 Do my homework.

29

The final bell rings.
"Well," he says grandly, shaking my hand,
"This is it."
I laugh and say,
"You'll be fine!"

Oh, Father, please let him be fine.
Guard him from fear and loneliness.
Oh, send an angel home with him.

For the Child Who Adores Me

Lord,
I'm writing this from the top of a pedestal.
Just why she placed me here,
I'll probably never know.
But here I am,
gulping the rarified air
and feeling a little rocky
as she gazes up at me,
unnervingly like a cocker spaniel.
Oh, dear.
I don't deserve this.
I mean, I *really don't deserve* this!
It's flattering, people tell me
in kindly amusement,
to have earned somehow
the admiration of a child.
But Lord, this kid likes me so much
she makes me nervous.
I'm afraid that someday
I'll inadvertently hurt her,
her love is so raw.

30

Oh, Lord,
I'm writing this from the top of a pedestal.
Show me a way
to step down gracefully
before I topple off.

For the Child Who Doesn't Like Me

I honestly don't understand it, Lord.
I don't know why she doesn't like me.

How do I know she doesn't?
Little things, I guess.
You know I don't take sass, Lord,
but she saunters along the edge.
She pushes as hard as she dares
against any rule she can.
She looks irritated when I praise her work—
as if, who am I to be saying these things?
And she doesn't—
well, it sounds kind of petty,
but she doesn't laugh at my jokes.
On purpose!

Little things, you know?
But they rattle me.
They rattle the precious image I hold
of myself
as some kind of pedagogical Pied Piper.
When you're a grown-up, a teacher,
and a kid doesn't like you,
it's downright embarrassing.

31

I try to be reasonable.
I think to myself, "It's simple.
We just have a personality clash."
But then I think,
"Where does she get off having a personality?
At least one that clashes with mine?"

So I don't know, Lord.
Where do we go from here?
If you could just somehow keep my chagrin
from sliding into anger and unfairness.
And if you could just somehow help her learn,
in spite of her feelings for me.
And if you could just somehow—

Oh, Lord, I wish she'd come on over.

For the Chatterbox

Father,
one day, several years ago,
this child said his first word,
and so far the novelty hasn't worn off.
He's not a bad kid, Father.
He's not even all that noisy.
He's just so *incessant*—
chattering away to anyone and everyone
and on and on and on and on.
I've moved his seat so many times,
his desk should be on casters.
In desperation,
I banished him to the far corner of the room,
where he struck up a conversation
with the gerbils.

Father, I pray for peace and quiet.
No, not just for my sake,
but for his sake, too.
For there is a time to speak,
but there is also
a time to listen,
a time to reflect,
a time just to be
still.

So, Father, I don't ask that you take away
his gift of the gab.
But rather I ask
that you quiet him with your love
and let him receive, sometimes,
the gift of silence.

For the Restless Child

Lord,
this child
with her fidgets and wriggles
    and jiggles and joggles

(Just now
    she
        fell
            out
                of
                    her
                        chair!)

33

is frazzling my
   jangling my
   jarring my
    N$_E$R$_V$E^S!!!

Gentle Shepherd,
lead us both to calmer waters . . .

For the Child Who Fights

Father, this child glares at the world
through sullen eyes
and comes out swinging.
I'm not praying for understanding.
I understand him all too well.
He is every-man-for-himself.
He is look-out-for-number-one.
He is the-voice-of-anarchy-
   in-a-world-gone-mad.
He is me.
(Or my baser instincts, anyway.)
Oh, Lord,
I *want* my classroom to be
a cradle of civilization.
I *want* to be a wise and gentle teacher
showing this child a Better Way.
But mostly I want to kill him.
He brings out the vigilante in my soul.
That's because it's hard to be wise and gentle
when I'm hauling someone out of line
for kicking.
For the fourth day in a row.
I have this fantasy

34

(and so far it's only that!)
of bouncing him against the wall
and screaming,
"When will you ever learn
that 'people are not for hitting'?
Take *that!*"
Splat!
No, Lord, I'm not praying for understanding.
I understand his angry spirit all too well.
I'm praying for . . .
Father, there's this other teacher I know of.
And, oh, what I wouldn't give
for even a little of his quiet strength,
his calm restraint!
He met this problem of violence, too,
and he could have wiped out the offenders.
With ten thousand angels.
But he didn't.

Lament

For John P.
Born—February 10, 1971
Died—December 20, 1978

Oh, Father, how the images come back to me!

At the Christmas party
he stood beneath the bright piñata,
blindfolded, swinging a plastic bat,
all energy and concentration,
intensely alive.

35

In less than an hour, he was dead.
Drowned. He fell through the ice
on his way home from school
for Christmas vacation.

On that first day back
I came in early to pack his things
and remove his desk
before the kids
could see it there,
so achingly empty, alone.

And the room was filled
with overwhelming sadness.
All silence—save for the voice of Rachel,
weeping for her children.

For the Child from Another Language and Culture

Lord, before I met her, I thought, "Oh, great!
I don't know how I'll deal with this—
to get a kid who's new to this country,
who speaks no English,
whose name I can't even pronounce.

How will I cope?"

But then
with what sweet courage she
walked into our babble.
And coped.

For the Child Whose Family Is Going Through a Divorce

Father, his family is going through a divorce,
and I'm supposed to watch him
for signs of strain.
Fighting with peers.
Crying at the slightest provocation.
Resisting authority.
Neglecting schoolwork.
Things like that.
His world is simply coming apart,
and I'm supposed to watch him
for signs of strain.

And what can I do to help him? I ask.
Offer him comfort and support, I'm told.
But how can he receive that from me?
Because to accept my help
would be to accept the awful truth.
He wants his family back together again.
No more. No less.
And I, only his teacher,
wonder helplessly
when to clamp down
and when to ease up.
And in the meantime watch him
for signs of strain.

Oh, Lord, how can we ever say it—
that children are "resilient,"
"able to recover quickly
from illness, change, and misfortune"?

37

If they are at all,
it is only through a *miracle* of grace.
But forgive us, forgive us, forgive us
for speaking glibly,
for belittling their pain.
It's just that we adults are showing
signs of strain.

For the Abused Child

Oh, God, hear me!
He says he got the bruises last night
when he fell down
in the bathtub
or was it the stairs
he says he doesn't remember which
but I know as surely as if I'd seen it all
that that's not what happened.
Oh, God. Oh, God.
Why is this happening?
They told us it might
they told us
to check.
I didn't really think it would ever happen
but even so
I accepted the mandate
because it was a mandate
and that's what we're supposed to do
so I put it on my list, you know,
so matter-of-factly
because I couldn't handle it any other way:
just the routine—

PRAYERS FOR THE CHILDREN

collect the lunch money
take attendance
lead the pledge
notice bruises . . .
Oh, God.
Let me think.
Okay. Get help.
I have to see the principal.
This kid, this . . .
I have to pray for him,
I have to pray,
but my thoughts lie heavy in my mind,
groaning like some poor wounded thing.
Oh, God.
This little boy.
Why am I so afraid?
And the principal stares at me,
mutely catching my alarm
behind the words,
"Um, could you come take a look
at one of my kids?
I think we might have a problem here."

On the Forgiving Spirit of Children

Oh, Father, I get so discouraged sometimes.
I brood about how irritable and unreasonable I have been.
And I think, if I had been a kid in my class today,
would I want to come back tomorrow?

But tomorrow they are there,
and—miraculously—they are glad to see me.

Young children are the most forgiving people in your
    world, Father.
Even to seventy times seven.
And their generosity
is the antidote for my discouragement.
For they trust me enough
to let me start again.
And I love them enough
to want to try again.

Because of them
I glimpse your love,
which bears all things,
believes all things,
hopes all things,
and endures all things.
Bless us, Father, as we follow your example
and forgive one another in love.

Jesus and the Children

Oh, Lord Jesus,
some days I wonder what you saw in them.

How could you gather those whiny, crabby little humans
in your arms
and bless them?
Did they push and shove to get to you,
or worse yet,
take cuts in line?
Did they tattle on their best friend
or ruthlessly tease the victim of the week?
That's the reality of kids, Lord.

Oh, but help me to remember
that no less real
is their curiosity, their open-heartedness, their zest.
Nowhere but in children
do we see such receptive, eager, and humble learners.

So, Lord Jesus,
remind me what you saw in them:
the very kingdom of heaven.

In Praise of Children

Lord, you have made these children
as varied as the flowers of a garden.
You have blessed each one uniquely.
And each fragile, growing child
is infinitely precious in your sight.
You have trusted me to nurture them.
And blessed me with the joy of seeing them grow.
Lord, I teach in reverence.

PART 2

PRAYERS THROUGHOUT THE YEAR

It is the supreme art of the teacher to awaken joy in creative expression and knowledge.

Albert Einstein

At the Summer Workshop

For Bill Martin, Jr.

In July,
my group wrote poems on paper rainbows.
Another group played tambourines
and sang, with brimming hearts,
"The Grand Old Duke of York."
The leader beamed and called us by the name
Good Teachers.

In July,
September seems so far away.

Come September, there'll be seating charts
and worksheets, attendance books,
permission slips, referrals . . .
But, Father, let there always be

Tambourines! Poetry!

At the Teacher's Supply Store

Father, help me.
It's the middle of August.
I'm standing outside the teacher's supply store.
And I feel a spree coming on.
A smiling purple dinosaur (what else?)
calls to me from the window,
his speech balloon filled
by the two magic words:
"Welcome Back!"

44

Yes, it's that time again when teachers go
BACK TO SCHOOL!
And all of a sudden I'm
READY!
But that doesn't mean
I have to go crazy in there,
does it, Father?
I mean, do I really need:
    a rubber stamp smiley face that says,
      "Oops! Try again!"?
    a storytelling apron?
    a thirty-seven-inch birthdays calendar?
    a packet of origami paper?
    a packet of *any* flavor scratch-and-sniff stickers?
    a five-pound bag of plaster of Paris?
    a whole blackline-masters book on silent *e?*
Remind me, Father, of the value
of moderation.
Oh—and don't let me forget
to pick up one of those purple dinosaurs.

After Waking Up from a School Nightmare

I lie in the darkness,
the fear receding,
the relief of wakefulness flooding in.
It was only a dream.
It was only a dream.

But, Father, it's always the same dream.
I'm late and I'm lost,
rushing through vaguely familiar corridors,
clutching desperately at my armload

45

of falling papers,
unable to find my own classroom.

Then suddenly
I'm there.
I throw open the door.
But it's too late.
The kids have gone wild.
And I can't stop them—
not with any
"classroom management" technique.
Everything has spun
hopelessly, wildly, totally
out of control.

Oh, Father, where does it come from—
this irrational terror of the night?
No matter.
In a few hours it will be morning.
All balance will be restored.
And I will be my rational self again—
a person who day after day
for hours on end
shuts herself alone in a room
with twenty-seven children.

In My Classroom the Week Before School Starts

Awakened by the scrape
of my chalk, the room looks about
for the children.

On the Night Before School Starts

School starts tomorrow, Lord, and I'm nervous.
Ease my anxiety.
Give me confidence,
and let my confidence give the children security.

Let my external control
be a means of promoting their inner control,
so that classroom order
becomes a shared responsibility.
Let me have the kind of self-control
that teaches by example.

And let my discipline be patterned after yours,
rooted in a love
that will settle for nothing less than their best.

School starts tomorrow, Lord; make me ready.
You have given me a job to do
and the ability to do it well.
You have given me your promise that you will never
    leave me.
And you have guided me in all my preparation.

So now let me face tomorrow
eagerly and unafraid,
for ultimately my confidence rests in this:
"I am ready for anything
through the strength of the one
who lives within me" (Phil. 4:13 PHILLIPS).

On the First Day of School

It's the first day of school, Lord,
the beginning of a school year as fresh
as the children's slick, unopened notebooks
and newly sharpened pencils.
It's the first day of school,
and already I'm mentally exploring the new year,
wondering whether I'll see the familiar landmarks
I've seen in years past.

Will September again be the rocky period of adjustment
when we must settle the question of who's in charge here?

Will October again see routines well established
before the onset of Halloween hysteria?

Will November again see the class suddenly "jell"
and begin to function as a group?

Will Christmas again come all too quickly?

Will January see achievement levels spread far apart,
with some children off and flying,
and others barely started?

Will February ever end?

Will March produce another crop of late bloomers?

Will April bring my usual case of springtime regrets
and anxieties over work yet undone?

Will May bring the same restless euphoria?

48

Will June bring the same ambivalent feelings—
rejoicing at the arrival of summer,
yet regretting the departure of the children?

It's the first day of school, Lord,
and the year ahead seems reassuringly predictable.
But, while I guess at what this year might bring,
only you know what it will bring.
Only you know the future,
with all its problems
and joys.
God of all our days, I commit this year to you.

Before the Class Comes Marching In

Well, Father, what do you think?
The room looks nice, doesn't it?
Breathe in. Breathe out. Relax. Relax.
Today is the first day of school.
And—depending on the class I get—
today *could* seem
like the first day of the rest of my life.
That's the funny thing about classes,
isn't it, Lord?
I mean, the *Class*
seems to have a personality all its own,
in addition to all the personalities in it.
The whole being greater
than the sum of its parts, and all that.
What do you think—
the room looks nice, doesn't it?
I've been thinking about it a lot, Lord,
and there are two messages

49

I want to get across right from the start:
  "Welcome, child!
  I believe in you!
  Together we can have a delightful year
  of learning and growth!"
And
  "Nobody messes with me, kid!"
I think that just about covers it, Lord!
Breathe in. Br—
Oh! There's the bell.
Just one more thing, Lord.
You're not going anyplace, are you?

This Kid Has a Bad Reputation

There's a little boy coming in the door, Father.
It's only the first day of school,
but I already know a lot about him.

From his records I know that,
while his I.Q. is above average,
his "degree of consistency of effort on study assignments
has been unsatisfactory."
An underachiever.

I also know that he has "exhibited a lack of acceptance
of reasonable authority."
A discipline problem.

His reputation precedes him.
Even as he walks through the door,
I know all about him.

But, gracious Father,
in your lovingkindness you designed the perfect gift
for imperfect human beings: a fresh start.
And it is a gift you bestow
as often as we come to receive it.

Mistakes need not be cumulative;
each day can be a new beginning.
Father, freely I have received;
now let me freely give.
There's a little boy coming in the door
who could use a fresh start.

On the Night of Open House

"Hello!
Yes, please come in!"
    Another Open House, Father,
    and it doesn't get any easier,
    awkwardly welcoming curious strangers
    into my little room-world.
"Please feel free to look around."
    I risked my life hanging those
    paper bag owls
    from the ceiling,
    and they'd better notice them.
"'How is she doing?'
Oh, fine—
but, actually, it's a little early in the year
to tell much . . ."
    Help me, Lord!
    Which one is theirs?
    I don't have all the last names down yet.

51

"Jimmy!
How nice that your little brother
gets to see your room!"
    Who let all these preschoolers in?
"But you must explain to him
that he can't go in the science corner
where we worked so hard
to set up our display!
How old is your little brother?"
    Good! I have time to apply for a transfer.
"And you're Michael's parents?
Of course!
I certainly see a family resemblance!"
    Yes, Lord, this explains a lot!
"What's that? Cindy
talks about me all the time?
Ha-ha. Nice things, I hope."
    Good grief, Lord, what does she say?
"I'm so glad to have had this chance to chat with you."
    *Lord, please make Jason's parents
    stop talking.
    There's a line of other parents
    waiting to meet me,
    and I feel like a duchess
    at a diplomatic reception.
    Except that my feet hurt.
    And I just want to go home
    and watch TV.*
"Oh, yes, I agree with you.
It's always good to be able to put a face with the name."
    *Oh, Father, what do they think of me?
    I'm a nice person—albeit a touch
    ill at ease tonight.*

52

*And they're nice people—also ill at ease
as they peek into the world
I share with their children,
so apart from the world
they share with them at home.*

"I do appreciate your taking time
to come out tonight.
We're looking forward to a great year!"
   And that's the truth.

During the Excitement of Holidays

Father,
thank you for jack-o'-lanterns
and brown sack turkeys,
for cotton-bearded Santas
and paper doily valentines.

Thank you for holidays,
and for the love of life
and renewal of creativity
they inspire.

Thank you for children
and for their contagious sense of festival.
Father,
bless this day for them;
and for their teacher,
an extra measure of grace?

* *

On the Night of the Big Program

Oh, they're all decked out
    In their antlers and bells—
Supposed to be reindeer.
    (Can anyone tell?)

Their spirits are high;
    They're full of good cheer.
(Which is trying the patience
    Of some of us here.)

"Okay, everybody, line up—
    And don't crowd.
Don't fall off the bleachers;
    Just sing nice and loud."

(That tune, learned in Music
    In time for tonight,
Will ring in my brain
    For the rest of my life.)

"And then, when your part of the concert
    Is done,
We'll wait in our classroom."
    (Won't *that* be fun.)

Lord, they're all so excited
    At being out late,
At having the spotlight . . .
"Wow! You guys did GREAT!"

54

When a Child Leaves in the Middle
of the Year

Father,
it's hard to describe her mood today.
Already she stands a little apart from us.
She's edgy, I guess,
and oddly subdued.
Eager to be off,
to start over,
to get the good-byes behind her,
yet so reluctant to let go and leave us.

We, too, are reluctant.
How hard it is
to think of someone we know
and like so much
being a stranger in a new place,
    entering a classroom that is not ours,
    sitting among classmates who are not these,
    greeting a teacher . . .

There's something unfinished
about this, Lord!
June . . . *June* . . . not January,
is the time for good-byes.
June—when they all leave together,
not January—with this one little piece of us,
broken off,
leaving alone.

She cleans out her desk
and turns in her books.

55

We have a party in her honor.
Her mother comes early
to pick her up.
I walk them to the classroom door.
A little too brightly I say,
"Remember your promise to write to us!"
She nods
and hugs me, quickly, tightly;
then turns and hurries away.

Aching, my heart calls after her,
"Go with God!"

When It Might Be a "Snow Day"

Wow, it's really coming down out there, Lord!
But when is too much snow
enough snow
to close the schools?
I can't imagine
they're going to have school today . . .
But it's 6:17,
and Peggy hasn't called me yet.
The superintendent calls the principal,
the principal calls Peggy,
Peggy calls me,
I call Marilyn and Gary . . .
It's really coming down!

Oh, Lord, I need a white day—
a day not scribbled up with lesson plans,
a day unmeasured by nerve-jarring bells—
a downy comforter of a day

a marshmallow day
a snow day.

On such a day
I might bake bread.
I might read a novel.
I might bake bread *and* read a novel.

But such a day cannot be taken
when school's going on without me,
and I'm not *really* sick enough to be home.
No, such a day
can only be given.
Oh, Lord, I need a snow day.

It's 6:38.
The telephone's ringing.
Oh, please, let it be Peggy.
Oh, please, please, please, please, please!

In the Middle of a Long, Dull Stretch

Father,
I confess that the prospect of another day
stretching before me
is a burden,
rather than a joy.

I've lived these past few weeks
in a state of mental and emotional malaise,
going routinely about my work,
without those sparks of creativity and spontaneity
that make life so exciting and satisfying.

57

The days are hectic,
crammed with pressures and demands,
but the hours pass slowly by—empty and barren.

Refresh me, Father.

Ease the tension that comes from boredom.

Show me how to bring vitality to a job that's gone stale.

Restore to me the absorbing joy of an artist at work,
for truly good teaching is an art.
Oh, Father,
you have given me time,
and you have given me skill.
Teach me to take delight in both,
using my time and my skill
to do something worthwhile,
to teach.

At Grading Time

There they sit, Father,
a neat stack of yellow report cards.
And here I sit,
an anxious and bewildered Solomon,
praying in my heart for wisdom,
while the controversy about grading surges on.

Should there be an objective standard
whereby children are measured against other children?

And how do we weigh a child's achievement
against his ability and effort?

Can we penalize a child for having little natural ability,
when he can't get a high mark
no matter how hard he tries?
And what about the child for whom A's come easily?
Will he skim through school never knowing what it is
    to try?

And what is happening
when an A becomes so important that a child will cheat
    for it,
perhaps to avoid abuse at home?

So here I sit, Father,
forced to take these cards seriously
because other people do.
Long on questions,
short on answers.

Father,
as I reach reluctantly for the top card,
let me also reach for your promise:
"If any one of you lacks wisdom,
let him ask of God
who gives to all men generously
and without reproaching,
and it will be given him" (James 1:5).

When My Class Is the Pits

Remind me, Lord, this, too, shall pass.
This class
shall pass.

59

When a Child Is Going to Be Retained

Him: I flunked.

Me: No, you didn't "flunk." We talked about this before, remember? Your parents and I agreed that you need to repeat this grade.

Him: I flunked.

Me: Don't think of it like that. Think of it as getting a second chance. And if you work hard next time around, you'll catch up on all the stuff you didn't learn this year. *Then* you'll be ready to move on!

Him: I flunked.

Me: No, no, no. Please stop saying that.

But you know what, Father?
This kid flunked.
He's not being held back
because he's developmentally unready
or because he was ill
and missed a lot of school.
He's being held back
because he didn't do a lick of work all year.
He flunked.
And he needed to say that.
And I wouldn't let him.
In an effort to make him feel good
about himself,
I denied him the right
to feel bad about himself.
Oh, Father, it's a hard truth—
no adult can *make* a kid learn anything.
But when he said he flunked,
I told myself
I flunked.

60

So I wanted to rush him through
the valley of the shadow of failure
and out into the bright sunlight
of a new beginning.
Before he was ready.
I'm sorry.
He flunked.
He well and truly flunked.
And he has the courage to see it and name it.
And with courage like that,
maybe he'll turn his life around.
Wouldn't that be something?
Oh, wouldn't that be something?

The Child I Never Got to Know

It's become my end-of-the-year observance,
Lord, to place their composite picture
before me and look again at all those faces
as yet unformed, endearingly scruffy,
so alike, yet not the same.

I see again the kid so secretly dear
to my heart I wanted to smuggle him home
in my bag. And here's the kid who
so drove my mind to distraction I saw his
impish grin in ceiling cracks.
But here—

here I feel a sudden pang at the face
of the child I never got to know.
I ask myself how it can be that she remains

as much unknown to me now as then—
almost a stranger.

I wish attention were like cupcakes, Lord,
with exactly enough to go around—
no one getting too much or too little.
Oh, may she get extra attention next year!
Lord, I feel the loss of her! Does she
of me?

On the Last Day of School

Father,
a quiet tension fills the room
on this last day of school.
I expected exuberance and rowdiness,
but that came yesterday,
when there was still one day to go.
Today the children are disturbingly subdued.
I am embarrassed at my own emotions;
I cannot look at the children directly.

The room is so blank.
Our desks are cleaned out.
The last traces of the party have been swept away.
The charts and posters are down for the summer.

So now we sit quietly,
too wrought even for songs and games,
and we wait for the bus to come.

I expect to see these children again, of course,
but it won't be the same.

They know it,
and I know it.

They will come around to see me,
jealous of the new class,
and I will look at a room of little strangers
and miss the familiar faces.

In time
the strangers will become friends.
But every class is different and special;
no new group of children will ever take the place
of the one leaving me today.

Lord,
I have worked hard,
and I have loved these children dearly.
In investing in their future
I have cast my bread upon the waters,
content that I will find it after many days.

Lord, I commend them into your hands.

PART 3

PRAYERS FOR
SPECIAL TIMES

*Life is amazing; and the teacher had better prepare himself to be
a medium for that amazement.*

Edward Blishen, *Donkey Work*, Part 2, Chapter 5 (1983)

Sunday Night Insomnia

Oh, Father,
how is it possible
to be so wearied and so wired
all at the same time?
The luminous numbers glare at me
as if to say,
"Aren't you sleeping *yet?!*
How do you expect to get up for school
in the morning??"
Yet that's what's keeping me awake—
having to get "up" for school.

How much easier Monday morning would be
if I could just shuffle over to my desk
with a cup of coffee and a doughnut,
write out my to-do list in peace,
piddle about with some papers,
ease myself into the week.
How much simpler teaching would be
if the kids didn't arrive
until sometime around Tuesday afternoon.

But Monday morning they are there—
bright-eyed and bushy-tailed,
spilling book club money out of their mittens,
chattering away to me
in dialogue straight from
the theatre of the absurd:
"You know what?
Yesterday we went by my grandma's?
But one of the fish was dead!"

Oh, Father,
I need some sleep.
I'm a teacher.
I don't have the luxury
of a sluggish Monday morning.
If anything,
I have to be brighter and bushier than they.
I am, after all, Head Squirrel.
At what point did I stop making sense?
Maybe this means I'm drifting off.
Father,
I have to get up for school tomorrow.
And I need your gifts
of strength
and peace.
And sleep.
I need some sleep . . .

On the Day of the Field Trip

Father, we're going on a field trip this morning,
and I would ask that you . . .

Excuse me a minute, Father,
someone just said that the buses are here . . .

All right, it's time to line up.
Find your partners, please.

Have to count noses one more time, Father.

All set? Then, let's go. Walk, Christopher.

67

Oh, Father, about Christopher,
please don't let him . . .

> *All right, children.*
> *Please remember that your bus number is 120.*
> *That way, if you get separated from your group*
> *at the museum*
> *you'll be able to find the bus*
> *in the parking lot.*
> *Of course, you're not going to get separated*
> *from your group,*
> *but if you do,*
> *your bus number is 120.*
> *Now, let me hear you say it, 120.*

Oh, Father,
please don't let me lose any of them.

> *Christopher, put your name tag on, please.*
> *You absolutely must wear your name tag.*

Let me catch my breath, Father.
They're all safely on the bus,
and we're ready to roll.

> *Scoot over, Christopher,*
> *I'll sit beside you, I think.*
> *Yes, yes. You can have the window.*

Whew, Father.
Where was I?
Oh, yes.
Please help me to relax and have a good time.

I don't know why, but suddenly I remember a prayer
Sir Jacob Astley, the Puritan general,
once prayed:

> "Lord, Thou knowest we must be busy today.
> If we forget Thee,
> do not Thou forget us."

Amen, Father,

Amen.

When the Whole Class Flunks the Test

Father,
I'm sorry I yelled at them like that,
I really am.
It's just . . . I mean . . .
how could this *happen?*
Sure, I expected a few would mess up,
but *all* of them?
I honestly thought they were getting it!
What were we doing all that time?
All my creative song-and-dance,
all my review and hard-nosed drill,
how could it come to . . . to nothing?
HOW CAN THEY NOT KNOW
THIS STUFF??

Father,
I'm not sure I even want
what I'm about to ask for,
but here goes:

Insight (to know what went wrong)
Wisdom (to find a better way)
Patience (to—oh, help us!—try again)
Perspective (it isn't, I guess,
the end of the world)
Oh, and toss in a little humor, too, okay?
(I could sure use some!)

During the Fire Drill

The buzzer went off during math,
startling us so much
we couldn't for a moment
think what it was.
"Fire Drill," I said firmly.
"Line up quietly
in ABC order.
No talking.
No running.
No shoving or pushing.
Last one out,
turn off the lights
and close the door.
All set?
Let's go."

Oh, Father, is there anything more annoying
than a fire drill?
We couldn't stop for our coats, of course,
and it's too cold to be out here without them.
The kids are hopping up and down
and flapping their goose-pimply arms,
looking for all the world

70

like, well, goslings.
So cute and funny.
And suddenly,
so overwhelmingly
dear.
So vulnerable.

I guess that's what I hate about a fire drill:
It makes me think,
What if?
What if there were a real fire?
Could I get the kids out safely?
Would our wing
(as per the instruction leaflet)
exit quickly and calmly
by the northwest door?
I hate hearing about disasters—
about fires and floods and earthquakes
and tornadoes,
the sound of the whole creation groaning,
reminding us that we live in a fallen world.

But worst of all
are the evils we make for ourselves.
Oh, Father,
from hunger
and violence
and war
and poverty
and illiteracy
and injustice
give us the grace to protect our children,
all the children of the world.

"Hey! The other classes are going in now!"
The children stare at me
in uneasy bewilderment
as I swallow hard
and fumble for a Kleenex.
"All right, let's go,"
I say more gruffly than I mean to.
"No running.
No pushing or shoving.
Someone could get hurt."

When I Get Flak

Deliver me from my enemies, O God.*
    Enemies!
    What am I doing with enemies?
    What is the matter with these people?
    This is the first I knew
    anything was wrong!

Protect me from those who rise up against me.
    It seems one of them
    didn't like
    the way I graded some papers.
    (Or something like that.
    I'm not sure I follow it all.)
    So she phoned all the other parents
    and led a stormy little group of them
    straight to the principal's office.

*Selected verses from Psalm 59 (NIV), a psalm of David when Saul had sent men
to watch David's house in order to kill him.

I have done no wrong,
   Lord, you know I don't deserve this!
   From a molehill of a misunderstanding
   she has churned up a mountain of spite.

yet they are ready to attack me.
   Why?
   Why are they ready to attack me?
   I work so hard!
   I care so much!
   Is this how they pay me back
   for all the love I've given their kids?

Arise to help me; look on my plight!
   My plight
   is that I'm hurt and bewildered.
   (How could they do this to me?)
   Unsure of myself.
   (Do I really know what I'm doing?)
   Lonely.
   (Other teachers get this, too, right?
   Right?)
   And so mad I feel sick.

O my Strength, I watch for you;
you, O God, are my fortress, my loving God.
In the morning I will sing of your love;

because I think today
is pretty much shot.

At the End of a Good Day

Father, today I felt your presence in the classroom.
By faith I know that you are always there,
but thank you for those times that *confirm*
that in you we live
and move
and have our being.

Father, today it all felt so *right*.
The children were joyously absorbed
in what they were learning,
and I moved among them
full of the satisfaction of a job well done.
Thank you for those times of quiet joy
when it is good just to be.
Thank you for gently reminding me
that you have brought the children and me together
for a purpose,
and that the work you have given me to do
is a sacred trust.

On a Rainy Day

"Is that any way to start the morning?"
I yell at the two children
I have just relegated to opposite ends of the room
for fighting.

Father, the first bell just rang,
and already this day has all the makings of a disaster.

74

The steady downpour of rain shows no sign
of letting up.
And, sensing that they will be indoors all day,
the children are busy practicing being restless and noisy.

The latest mandate from the office means one thing—
more paperwork.

Five children are trying to talk to me at once.

I shush them while I try to arrange the mounds
of miscellaneous paper on my desk into
neat mounds of miscellaneous paper.

The five children persist
and at last are able to communicate
that Sharon just threw up.
Somehow, I am not surprised.

Is this any way to start the morning?

Father, stop me.
Stop me from declaring this day a disaster
before it's even begun.

Save me from wasteful anxiety
over things I can't control,
and help me to work on something that only I can
    control—my attitude.

Father, this is a day that you have made.
Help me to rejoice and be glad in it.
This is a rainy day that you have made.
Help me to relax and take it a little at a time.

75

In the Middle of a Bad Day

Father,
help me to recognize a bad day for what it is—
a day.
It does not represent the rest of the year,
or the rest of the month,
or even the rest of the week.
Keep me from making value judgments based on this day.
Keep me from deciding that the children are hopeless,
that my work is in vain,
and that I am a failure.

Oh, Father,
I'm discouraged and tired today,
but I'm not a failure.
I'm disorganized and frazzled today,
but the classroom still functions.
I'm impatient and crabby today,
but the children know I love them.

It's a bad day today,
but it's only a day.
It will pass.
Give me the patience to wait it out,
and to hold my letter of resignation
until tomorrow!

When My Class Is the Greatest

Father, sometimes I call them to line up, and
trailing clouds of glory do they come
from the playground,
not quarreling,
but laughing and eager
to get back to work.
And sometimes I can't believe
how good they are.
And I think,
"This is it.
This is what it's all about.
And I can walk with kings,
because I am a *teacher*
and these are my sweet, beautiful students!"
But then I think,
"They've got to be up to something, right?"

On the Morning of the Standardized Test

MEMO TO: The Test-makers, Somewhere in Iowa or California
(I forget which)
FROM: A Teacher
RE: Your Standardized Test
DATE: Day of Administering Said Test

As you know, my school district spent a lot of money on your test, and therefore must take the results very, very seriously. This is a mistake. I'm writing to protest the unfairness of it all.

It is first and most importantly unfair to the children. There's something inside us all (the image of God, perhaps?) that objects to being scored and ranked. I recall one year the little boy who took one look at your test, burst into tears, and threw it on the floor. You gotta admire perception like that.

It's unfair to teachers, for we will be judged by a school district grasping at scores. Now, if you've ever seen a kid . . . clutching a number 2 pencil . . . trying to color in the tiny oval . . . the *right* tiny oval . . . you'll appreciate why we're nervous.

It's unfair to the whole noble idea of Learning. Some districts, desperate for higher scores, have ordered teachers to teach the test. Only the test. Well, your test doesn't cover everything, and there are some things in life (perhaps most things of value) that can't be measured by a test at all.

It's time to get started. Your test manual instructs me to "Say: Good Morning," so I'd better go do that. I have just one more quick memo to write first.

MEMO TO: My Wise and Loving Heavenly Father

It's all so unfair, Lord. But I don't want to add to that unfairness. I want the kids at least to be able to give it their best shot. Help me, Father. Help me to do the best I can with something I don't believe in.

At the Teachers' Workshop

From theories and studies,
long-winded devotees,
and things that go clunk in the class,
Good Lord, deliver us.

After Hearing That a Child's Parent Has Died

Father,
the principal was just here to give me the news.
Johnny's mother
just died in an automobile accident.
I only nodded when he told me.
Now I turn back to the room.

The children stare at me, knowing something is wrong—
terribly,
terribly
wrong.
I clear my throat,
"Get out your math books," I tell them.
"I'll write the page numbers on the board."
They do as they are told.

They listen to me, Father.
And soon I'll have to tell them.
They'll look at me, and listen,
but they will not understand.

And soon I'll have to talk to Johnny.
He listens to me, too.
I'll talk to him
and hope with all my being
that he doesn't ask me,
Why?

Because, oh, my God,
I cannot tell him
what I do not know.

After Losing My Temper

Oh, God,
he pushed me too far
this time—
right to the brink of my endurance.
But he didn't push me over
the brink;
I jumped.
Kicked my professional discretion aside
and jumped.

In the parlance of the trade,
I "overreacted."
Oh, God,
I let him have it.

And now,
sitting alone at my desk,
I hold a coffee cup in trembling hands
and wonder what will happen to me.
I fight down panic.
And the rage
that flares up
every time I think of that kid.
Oh, that kid!

And for every bit of rage I feel toward him,
I feel a double portion for myself;
how could I be so *stupid?*
And sinking down
through all my feelings,
settling like a rock,
is a little lump of shame.

Oh, Father,
I gather up my wretched little bundle
of anger, fear, and shame
and lay it at your feet.

When a Child Comes Back to Visit After Many Years

We sat at lunch around the table, Lord,
when another teacher, beaming,
came in and exclaimed, "What a boost!"

He was having a bad day
in a bad year with a rough bunch of kids
and little to show for all his time and work.

He'd been spending a frenzied lunch time
alone in his room
where the principal found him
and smiling said, "You have a visitor
waiting for you in the office; come on!"

The teacher, wondering, hurried there and saw
a gangly, awkward, eager teen-aged boy.
And flashing back eight years, he saw
and exclaimed, "Tony!"

The mother laughed with pleasure.
"Wow! I'm impressed!
Do you remember all of them like that?"
"Oh," said the teacher, "I couldn't forget—
not Tony!" But I might have, he thought,

81

the way I blank out on names.
By what grace did it come, was sent,
to my lips just now? "Tony!"

Eight years ago in the life of a child is forever.
Eight years ago
and a thousand miles to this meeting.

The mother laughed again and said, "You're all
he's talked about for months—
ever since we planned to come back home to visit.
'Will he still be there?' he asked,
'I have to go and see. Will he remember me?
Will he?'" The teacher remembered
a bright but struggling little boy for whom
the weight of the world was packed
in just two words: First Grade.

By what grace, the teacher wondered,
did I sense to kneel beside him long ago,
to rub his back and whisper
that it would be all right?
What angel restrained my anger at his tears?

Now Tony, tongue-tied, stood before his friend
and smiled that well-remembered,
winsome smile.
His mother said, "You see he's shy, still shy."
The teacher said, "I, too, am shy.
It's okay to be shy."
And shyly then they all shook hands.

The boy had asked a thousand times,
"Will he still be there?"
And the teacher thought, I was here!
I was here!

We sat at lunch around the table, Lord,
and thought about how much we influence
these lives.
Exultant thought!
Yet frightening, too.
Lord, help us not to be afraid,
but trusting, teach them by your grace.

Before Being Evaluated

Well, Father, I *am* a little nervous,
but an hour from now
it will all be behind me.
An hour from now
I'll look back and smile.
And I'll think with relief,
"Well, that wasn't so bad!
The lesson went smoothly,
the kids were attentive,
the principal was impressed.
Not bad at all."
An hour from now
it will all be behind me.
An hour from now
I'll look back and smile.

I hope.

After Being "Pink-Slipped"

I got the news today, Father.
It's not as if I hadn't been expecting it;
I had.
It's just that
somewhere,
in the dimmest corners of my mind,
where hope lives,
I thought it might not happen.

I thought funds,
manna-like,
would suddenly appear.
Not ample funds,
but adequate.
Funds to buy materials,
continue programs,
hire us all back.

It's not as if it's final, though,
it's not.
The word is,
"wait-and-see."

Wait-and-see.
Can anything be harder?
I'd almost rather *know*.
And just by knowing
squelch the anxious hope
that I'll be back. . . .

But, oh, Father,
let me be back.

Yes, of course,
I need the money,
but it's more than that—

I need, well—
me.
I'm afraid that if I lose my job—
I'll lose myself.

Oh, Father,
bear me through this awful time
of despair and hope.
Give me the stamina
to wait-and-see,
the strength to face whatever comes.
And give me—me.

My job is what I *do*,
not what I am.
And what I am is—yours.
Your child.
Your trusting child.

After the Gripe Session

I don't know who said it, Father,
but it's true:
"Nothing unites a people like a mutual foe."
The fact that taking lunch room duty
is only a little like marching off to World War II
is beside the point.
The unity is the important thing.

Oh, but it was exhilarating
out on the playground this morning, Father.
Exhilarating,
to put our petty differences aside,
join hands and hearts,
and raise our voices
in One Great Gripe.

The exhilarating unity!
The spirit of camaraderie!
The fun of the common cause!
It's the stuff of revolution!

To put our petty differences aside,
join hands and hearts,
and—

But then the recess bell rang, and
keyed up
wrung out
let down
we gathered our kids
and straggled back to our rooms
alone.

PART 4

PRAYERS FOR
THE TEACHER

I'm not a teacher: only a fellow-traveler of whom you asked the way. I pointed ahead—ahead of myself as well as you.

George Bernard Shaw

For the First-Year Teacher

The first-year teacher
looks a little lost, Father—
as if they might have forgotten
to tell her a few things
in teacher training.
They certainly forgot with me!
But I've picked up a bit of know-how
over the years,
and I'd like to pass along
what I've learned.

Dear First-Year Teacher,

Your training is not over; it's just beginning. A good teacher must first and always be a learner. And you learn to teach by teaching. There is no other way.

So you must come to your first job now with both humility and confidence—humility because you don't know it all, and confidence because you know more than you think you do.

As you've no doubt painfully discovered, teachers are not as valued and respected by our society as they should be. Well, the way to begin changing that is to first of all respect yourself and your work. Your work is of immeasurable and lasting importance. (How many people can say that?) And you have the heart and soul of a teacher. You're a professional. So begin, without being rigid, to develop a point of view, a personal philosophy of education. Then trust your instincts. Who knows better about what succeeds in your classroom than you?

A word about personality: As a teacher, you really need to have one. In fact, a touch of megalomania doesn't hurt. You need to come into the classroom each day with the attitude that "I'm the Teacher, and I'm in charge here." You don't have to be nasty about it, of course, but your presence has to be felt. After all, if *you're* not in charge of your room, who is?

A further word about personality: The one you have should be your very own, not someone else's. This means that you must organize your classroom in a way that fits you. For example, if you are quiet and serious, don't feel that you must suddenly become perky, just because you signed a contract. Kids require two things of their teachers—niceness and fairness. Beyond that, they're more than willing to adapt to who you are. You can return the favor. Learn the age-level characteristics of the grade. And study the developmental stages above and below, too. That way you'll know where your kids are coming from and where they're going. General characteristics can carry you only so far, of course; get to know the *people* in your class. It's an old maxim, but it bears repeating: You're not just teaching a class, you're teaching individuals in that class.

So get to know your kids and let your kids get to know you. Be yourself. And bring your enthusiasms into the classroom. Are you crazy about underwater photography and Abyssinian cats? Share that with your kids! They'll love you for it. And they'll start sharing of themselves, too.

Having covered Personality, we come now to the Pencil Sharpener. Why do they never tell you in teacher training how important the pencil sharpener is? I mean by this, of course, that you have to decide how you're going to handle Every Picky Little Thing. Can the children get up to sharpen a pencil any time they want to? Or are you going to have them line up by rows at specified times? It's up to you, of course, but the point is, you have to *think* about it; it won't just take care of itself. The details of classroom management can drive you crazy. But if your "Rules for Our Room" doesn't look like the Manhattan yellow pages, you probably haven't covered everything.

89

Don't be dismayed if you find yourself saying no a lot more than you'd like to. It's all because you have this *group*. Sure, you'd like to tell the individual kid he can stretch his legs and get a drink of water, but if you do, you could be killed in the stampede.

Speaking of the group, it's very important to accept the class you get. This doesn't mean that you won't work with them or push them to do and be their best. But it does mean that thou shalt not covet thy neighbor's class because she has higher reading groups and few behavior problems. Your kids are *your* kids.

Never let yourself slip into a Them-against-Me mentality. While a classroom may be more like a benevolent dictatorship than a democracy, you *are* all in this learning-thing together. Don't start thinking that the kids are out to get you. They're not.

Having said that . . .

You will from time to time have *absolutely rotten* days. And if a nonteaching friend says in bewilderment, "They're just little kids; how bad can they be?" don't even try to explain.

Naturally, some of your best friends will be teachers because you all understand what the world of school is like. But important as it may be to talk through your teaching experiences, be careful not to rehash your days. Talk about something else sometimes!

It's easy to feel as a teacher, especially in your first year, that your job has swallowed you alive.

Let me explain why you're feeling overwhelmed. It's because you're overwhelmed. It's a best-kept secret, but let's bring it out in the open. There's no way in the world you can cover everything the state or local school district tells you that you have to cover. And it seems to be getting worse instead of better. How many times have you heard someone with a cause (maybe a perfectly good cause) say, "We've got to address this in our *schools*"?

So it all adds up to more hours than there are. This means that you have to set realistic goals and priorities. You can't do this all on your own. You have to get a feel from the principal and the other teachers as to what's most important, where to concentrate your time and effort.

Tune in to what the other teachers are doing around you, but be careful not to compare yourself too much with others. A topflight teacher can make you feel inadequate; a lousy teacher can make you feel smug. It's not just a matter of how many hours a teacher puts in, so don't set undue store by that. In every school there's someone who stays till six o'clock every night, and there's someone else who adamantly leaves at three o'clock carrying home nothing but her purse. Neither extreme is realistic, and somehow (through trial and error, I guess) you have to find what works for you.

Speaking of what works, we should say a word about curriculum. A healthy skepticism is in order. I once had a textbook manual tell me that while I was working with a small math group at the front of the room, another small group could be at the back of the room unsupervised, building a table. Nope.

Make careful lesson plans, but be prepared to "go with the flow."

That's because everything takes longer than it should. (If you allow fifteen minutes to carve the jack-o'-lantern, it will take fifteen minutes just to spread out the newspapers.)

That's because nothing takes up as much time as it should. (If you pass out paper-and-pencil puzzles to fill a dragging afternoon, two minutes later the kids will all be waving the thing in the air, yelling, "FIN-ISHED!")

You have to go with the flow because each teaching day is an experience unto itself, full of surprises. A bat in the multipurpose room, for example, is an interruption to be reckoned with. So you might as well do a mini-science lesson on bats.

But most of all, you have to go with the flow because your kids need you to attend to them. They might have something on their minds—any little thing from the "misty, moisty morning" to a snap-

91

shot of someone's new puppy. And it makes them restless until they've had a chance to be heard and have received an acknowledgement from you. So listen to your kids. And pay attention to the small stuff of life.

Teaching. Surely one of the toughest and most rewarding jobs in the world! What am I forgetting? Oh, yes. Don't skip lunch.

Well, Father,
that's what I've picked up
over the years.
I don't know if it will be
of any help to her.
But I *do* know this:
The most important help
any teacher can have
is a sense of your presence
in the everydayness
of classroom life.
The first-year teacher
looks a little lost, Father.
Watch over her.

For Renewal

Oh, Father!
The fights over who took whose pencil,
the pushing in the lunch line,
the papers turned in with no name,
the tattletales,
the whining,
the skinned knees,
the runny noses . . .

There's a starling
perched on the wire outside the window,
and I'd dearly love to trade places with him.
I understand more clearly than ever
mankind's yearning to fly.
Oh, to swoop away from all this!

Father, I can't fly away,
but I can be still.
I can be still and know that you are God.
You have called me to serve you as a teacher,
and while no one ever said teaching
was going to be easy,
you have promised to renew my strength.

I am envying a starling
when I could mount up with wings as an eagle:
"But they that wait upon the Lord
shall renew their strength;
they shall mount up with wings as eagles;
they shall run and not be weary;
they shall walk and not faint" (Isa. 40:31).

For Help in Listening

Father,
even as I talk to you now,
I affirm my faith
that you are listening.
You have assured us
that before we cry, you will answer,
while we are yet speaking, you will hear.

Father,
I confess that there is freer access to the throne of grace
than there is to my desk,
I cherish the privilege
of being heard by the Lord of the universe,
yet I am careless about listening
to the children in my class.
I am like the irresponsible servant
who expected better treatment
than he was willing to give.

The children are so eager to talk to me,
but I am often harried and aloof
as I go frantically about the business of teaching.

I suspect I am missing the point.

How much I could learn about the children,
about teaching,
about myself,
if only I would take the time,
and make the effort,
to listen.

Slow me down, Father.
Give me a heart that understands the importance
of a new pair of shoes
or a lost pencil.

If I have pressing matters at hand and must say,
"Not now, later,"
let me treat that as a solemn promise.

94

I expect the children to listen to me;
help me to listen to them.
Let me teach them by example
that one of the most generous and loving things
we can do for each other
is to "lend an ear."

So Father, forgive me my mistakes,
and strengthen me in my resolve to do better.
And, Father,
thank you for listening.

For the "Why Am I Not Doing Anything Important?" Blues

Oh, Father,
how small this world of the classroom is,
bounded by alphabet charts and chalkboards,
bookcases and maps.

And how far this world seems
from the adult circles of money and prestige.
While other adults work together in those circles,
I am alone
among a throng of scurrying, chattering little people.

Little people and little things.
My days are so filled with little things.

Today I handed out a ream of Kleenex,
marched a miscreant to the principal's office,
and put up a new bulletin board.

95

What am I doing here?
Why am I not doing anything exciting and important
in the grownup world?

But, Father, there were *other* "little things" today.

Today Kevin came up to me,
bubbling with excitement,
and said,
"I can read this whole book all by myself!"

Today Michelle wrote a story that said:
"My dog is brown and white. He is a very nice person."

Today Kathleen,
who has hardly said two words all year,
raised her hand to answer a question.

Perhaps years from now
I'll learn the results of these "little things"
that happened today.
Perhaps I won't.
But, Father, teach me to take delight in little things,
and never, never let me doubt their importance.

For Self-Acceptance

Father,
sometimes I think it might be easier
if she weren't in the classroom next door.
But then I think, No,
I'd still see her at the copier,
neatly running off and slipping into file folders

math papers she will need,
not in fifteen minutes,
but in three weeks.

I'd still see her in the lounge,
sipping a diet soft drink,
as she reads Piaget for fun.

I'd still see her
drifting perfumed and polished down the hall,
stopping only to tell a seven-foot-tall kid
to scrape his gum out of the drinking fountain—
and being obeyed.

But, oh—
first thing in the morning it *is* hard
to have her right next door.
Hard,
to come skidding down the hall,
and see her standing at her door
smiling serenely at her children as they arrive.
Smiling at her children.
First thing in the morning.

Oh, Father,
why can't I be like that?
You know, calm,
well-organized,
cheerful,
perfect?

I guess perfection's not my style.
You've helped me accept myself as a person—
imperfections and all.
So help me to accept myself as a teacher—
imperfections and all. Amen.

For Perspective

Father,
sometimes I think back to the videotapes
we saw in teacher training courses,
and I wonder what a tape of *my* classroom would show.

On some days, Father,
when I'm creative and energetic,
I think, "Let those cameras roll!"
Let them see a teacher
who drags out the brightly colored rods for a math lesson
instead of scribbling sketches on the board.
Let them see a teacher
who copes good humoredly
with children who eat paste.

That's on some days, Father.

On other days,
when I'm tired and at loose ends,
I shudder to think of anyone seeing me.
What a picture that would be, Lord.

There I am,
flapping my arms and screeching,
"Quiet, quiet, quiet!

Can't you children show a little SELF-CONTROL?!"

"O wad some Power the giftie gie us,
To see oursels as ithers see us."

But, "Thou, Lord, seest me."
You see me on the good days
and on the bad.
You know far more about my classroom
than a tape could ever show,
and you see me far more clearly
than I could ever see myself.
Yet, through it all,
inexplicably,
you go on loving me.
My good days have not earned your love,
and my bad days cannot diminish it.
Day by day, you go on loving me.

Lord,
help me to see myself more as you see me.
Help me to see the pattern of my days,
so that I am not puffed up by success
or cast down by failure.
Give me a sure and steady perspective.
Help me to know myself,
with all my strengths and weaknesses,
and with that knowledge, Father,
help me to grow.

For Confidence

Father,
I have this idea for something new.
(It's not in the Manual or anything;
it's just something I thought up myself.)
And I really think it might work.
It's just that I've never done
anything like it before.
Oh, I don't know.
Maybe I'd better not try it.
What do you think?

Yes, I *know* you've blessed me with
training, intelligence,
and drive.
It's just that
this idea I have—
well, it's not in the Manual or anything—
and it might flop . . .

Excuse me a moment, Father,
while I dig my hole a little deeper.
It's for this measly little talent.
Goodness knows, I don't have many,
and I want to be sure the one I have
is buried deep and safe. . . .

For Consistency

Father, you who are the same
yesterday,
today,

and forever,
help me to be consistent.

Help me to make my classroom a secure and stable place,
where the children know what I expect of them;
and what they can expect from me.

I pray that it might be said of my classroom that

nothing was ever promised that was not given,
nothing was ever threatened that was not carried out,
nothing was ever said that was not true,
nothing was ever taught that had to be unlearned.*

*Adapted from John Ruskin's reflections upon his home.

For the Substitute

Well, Father, here I am,
laid low with the flu,
and my thoughts are with my sub.

I have a few requests—
a sort of Substitute's Checklist,
because I've been there, Father, and I *know*.

☐ Please let her find the school.
It's in one of those new subdivisions
where hapless strangers have been known
to wander in,
valiantly searching for Pendragon Place,
never to return.

☐ Please banish from her thoughts
all memories of substituting stories

101

she has heard,
all tales of cherry bombs flushed down toilets,
wastepaper baskets set on fire,
chairs tossed from second-story windows.
It does no good to dwell on that.

☐ Please let her see on my desk
the names of the two most reliable kids—
the *only* two reliable kids—
I chose to be her "Helpers for the Day."
And please don't let them both have chicken pox.

☐ Please let her find the ladies' room.
(This is second only to finding the school.)

☐ Please give her a keen sense of judgment
when Billy says,
"My brother must have gotten my homework
mixed up with his.
May I go up to Mr. Whitaker's class
and get it, please?"
Billy has no brother.
And there is no Mr. Whitaker.

☐ And for the children, Father,
please give them the will to do their very best,
to treat the sub as if she were a welcome friend.
And gently bring to their minds
all I said I'd do to them
if I find their names
on a list
when I return.

When I'm the Teacher—Everywhere

Lord,
when the maitre d' asked,
"How many in your party?"
I answered, "FOUR!"
and held up four fingers.

But that's not all.

My answering machine
instructs the caller to sit up straight
and speak directly into the phone.

I circle the spelling mistakes
on supermarket flyers.

I switch off TV talk shows
when the speakers won't take turns
and raise their hands.

I just . . . I just . . .
want all the people in the whole world
to stay in their seats
and put their names on their papers.

Lord, help me.

For the Parent-Teacher Conference

We're both a little defensive, Father,
as we face each other across the desk.
I'm worried about what I'll say;
she's worried about what she'll hear;
and we're both worried about what the other is thinking.

Father, let her think kindly of me.
While she has primary responsibility for her child,
help her to know that he's very important to me, too.
In a sense, children belong to all of us,
and I invest a great deal of time, effort, and skill
in teaching the child who comes to me.

Father, let me think kindly of her.
Teach me how to know the difference between concern
    and nosiness.
Keep me from sitting in judgment—
automatically blaming her for her child's problems;
benevolently bestowing my advice.
Remind me that, while I have to cope with him for six
    hours a day,
she has to live with him.

We're both a little defensive, Father, so ease the tension.
Give us the problem-solving strength
that comes from working together.

For the Teacher Who's Going into Real Estate

Peggy turned in her letter of resignation
first thing this morning, Lord.
She won't be back, come fall.
And because rumor travels
at the speed of light
around this place,
everyone knew about it
before the second bell.

By some uncanny coincidence,
several of us led our bewildered classes
out to an extra-early recess
all at the same time.
Then, saying to our little hangers-on,
"GO PLAY!"
we settled down to the business at hand.

How could she do it? one of us demanded of Peggy. Such a good
teacher! How could she abandon the kids and the Cause of Education in America? But someone else interrupted to ask if Peggy's
office had any more openings. And someone else advised her to
keep her certificate current so that she could always come back.
Then someone else wondered aloud if it could be burnout—and
how do you know when you've had enough? And all of us agreed
that teaching is the hardest job there is and that it's harder than it
has to be. And why couldn't there be more clerical help and smaller
classes and more money and more . . . more *respect*?

And so it is
that Peggy's leaving teaching, Lord,
and going into real estate.
She won't be back, come fall.

For the Teacher Next Year

Father,
in her uncompromising scales I am weighed,
and, inevitably,
found wanting.

She says,
"Of course, the work I'm doing now
is work they should have gotten last year.
These children come to me knowing nothing."

I hasten to assure myself,
"That's not true."
But Father,
her arrow-sharp remarks
find their way home
to my insecurities and doubts
and cause more pain than I care to admit.

Father, if there's some truth in what she says,
help me to heed it.
If not,
help me to ignore it.
Relieve me of the anxiety and bitterness
this teacher's criticism brings.
Keep me from becoming petty and vindictive.
And do not let my defenses against unfair criticism
make me proud and unbending,
so that I cannot learn and grow.

Father, before you,
I am doing the best job I can.
Let me take comfort in that.
Amid the stress and conflict of life,
I have your firm and loving exhortation:
Fret not.
So help me to put my fretting aside
and get on with the work you have given me to do.

And when another teacher sends her children up to me,
help me to remember how much criticism hurts.

In Praise of Books

Today the children responded with open delight
as I read them a story
that was written over one hundred fifty years ago
and half a world away.
A story that was read to me
when I was their age,
every night, upon demand.

And now it is their turn, Father,
to receive this story in joy,
and claim it for their own.

What a marvel language is,
that it can freeze an author's thoughts and emotions,
and preserve them,
until they melt into the mind and heart
of a reader.

What a wonder words are,
that they can transcend space and time,
class and race,
uniting your sons and daughters
in literary fellowship.

Father, thank you for books.
Thank you for children.
And thank you for the delightful privilege
of bringing the two together.

In Praise of Learning

For reading;
that peculiar marks on a page are so able to inform us,
to entertain us,
and move us to laughter and tears,
we thank you, Father.

For handwriting, grammar and spelling;
which as tools enable us to capture our thoughts
and communicate them clearly to others,
we thank you, Father.

For mathematics;
with its dependable patterns and principles,
which reassure us that the world is not so inconstant
as we might fear,
we thank you, Father.

For science;
which challenges us to explore our universe
and reveals the world to be all the more wonderful
the more we understand it,
we thank you, Father.

For social studies;
which teaches us to know ourselves
and to know one another,
we thank you, Father.

For art;
with its absorbing, unexcelled joy
of making,
seeing, and appreciating the beautiful,
we thank you, Father.

For music;
with its mystical power to reach us
and unite us
as nothing else can,
we thank you, Father.

For physical education;
which teaches us to understand our bodies,
and gain satisfaction inherent in strength and skill,
we thank you, Father.

Father,
for all truth,
and for hearts and minds to know the truth,
we thank you.

In Praise of a Teacher

For Mr. Porter

One of our best teachers is retiring, Lord, and we've all been asked to offer a brief tribute. I want to say something glowing, something worthy of him, and the statement that comes to mind is this: He showed up.

That doesn't sound like much, I know. But I am reminded of a little girl I once knew who came home discouraged from her fist day at kindergarten. When her mother asked her what she had learned that day, she sighed and said, "Not much. I have to go back tomorrow."

How often we say that children grow up so fast, but that's not true. Growing up is a long, slow process, and kids need people who

109

will show up for them, to teach and nurture them—tomorrow after tomorrow after tomorrow.

Not everyone is willing or able to do that—to put so much into a job that offers so little in the way of money or perks or prestige. So why did he do it? For over forty years? Because he had this crazy, unshakable idea that kids are more important than anything else in the world. So he was a teacher, and he showed up.

On Showing Love

I found a note on the floor this afternoon, Father.
The children,
giddy with their newfound power over the written word,
have been ecstatically scribbling love notes
to each other and to me.

I found a note on the floor this afternoon, Father;
this one's addressed to you:

> *Dear God,*
> *I love you.*
> *Do you love me?*
> *Check one*
> *YES* □ *or NO* □

I smile at the request, but then,
oh, Father!
A sudden joy
wells up within me,
almost choking me
with its intensity,
when I think how abundantly
you have already checked, YES.

Checked our timid little question boxes
with your searing stroke of love.

Our loving Father.
Our matchless God.
For you exist—
and that would have been enough.
For you create—
and that would have been enough.
For you sustain—
and that would have been enough.
But that you should *love!*

Oh, God,
the heart of man cannot contain
the engulfing wonder of your love.

So let me not question
but receive.

Let your love well up within me.
Let it well up and spill over,
assuring the little one who wrote the note
and all who hunger in their hearts to know,
that the answer is Yes.

The answer is Yes.

PART 5

PRAYERS FOR PARENTS AND OTHER GROWN-UPS

A teacher affects eternity; he can never tell where his influence stops.

Henry Brooks Adams

For the Parents of a Gifted Child

Father, truly it must be unnerving
to have a child that smart,
to gaze on one's own offspring,
as they do,
with tickled awe.
We've met to decide what's best for him.
We, who don't know what to make of him.
Omniscient God,
what shall we do for this child?
Enrichment programs?
Private lessons?
Skipped grades?
Special classes?
His parents wonder what to give this boy
to whom so much has already been given.
But maybe there is still one thing.
And maybe it's something only they can give.
And maybe it's the smartest gift of all—
Childhood.

For the Parents of a Struggling Child

Father,
they come to the parent-teacher conference
warily,
wearily,
knowing full well
what they're not going to hear.
They won't hear
that their son is in the top reading group,
or that he's a whiz at math,

or that his penmanship is flawless,
or that he's entering the science fair,
or that he was last to sit down
at the spelling bee.

But Father,
let them hear what I have to say.

Let them hear
that even though school is hard for him
(and probably always will be),
he never gives up.
He struggles on until he gets it,
and what he's learned, he's *earned*;
it's his to keep.

Let them hear
that this report card doesn't mean
their son's not good enough.
Rather, this standard of measurement
isn't good enough to measure him.

Father,
let me say
and let them hear
that he's as fine and brave and good a person
as ever I've met.

They came this evening
warily,
wearily.
Let them go home satisfied
and proud.

115

For the Parent of a Coddled Child

He lifts her over the snowdrifts
when maybe the thing to do
is bundle her up,
wish her well,
and let her plow on through.

For the Troubled Parents

How shall I put it, Lord?
On the great worksheet of life,
these people don't color inside the lines.
They are,
in the parlance of the teachers' lounge,
the wacko parents,
the lunatic fringe,
who can make a teacher's life miserable.
So we laugh to help ourselves feel better.
But it's an uneasy laugh at best.
Because these are troubled people,
and their kids are growing up
in troubled homes.
We know we can't make the problem go away.
So we laugh.
Who can help them, Lord, but you?
Grant me the grace,
when I'm tempted to hold them in derision,
to hold them out to you
in prayer.

In Praise of Parents

There are people who faithfully save paper-towel rolls and cottage cheese containers (even when they hate cottage cheese) just because you've said you need them for "a project," and these same people never laugh at you or ask you why.

There are people who don a costume and march around the neighborhood in the Halloween parade, even though there's a good chance they'll run into somebody from the bank.

There are people who get plaques made of spray-painted macaroni shells for Christmas and who actually hang them on the wall.

There are people who stay up half the night arranging tiny red candy hearts into smiley faces on Valentine cupcakes.

There are people who hold bake sales and fun fairs and something called "pizza day" to raise money for computers.

There are people who take time off work to come to school for something called "career day," where they try to explain to a bunch of puzzled kids (their own included) what in the world they do for a living.

There are people who voluntarily climb on a bumpy school bus, where the decibel level can't even be measured, and ride 7,000 miles to the zoo. Then these same people—all in the name of education—accompany their little group into the ape house amid cries of "Eeewwwwww! It stinks in here! That one looks just like my brother! Eeewwwww! Do you see what he *did?*"

There are people who help with homework, sign report cards, run copies, who show up for the school play and applaud until their hands ache.

And then these same people tell you that you're doing a great job and that their kids love school because of you.

There are people called parents.

Thanks, Lord!

117

For the Principal

For Marv

You hear a lot of horror stories, Father,
and I know firsthand
that at least some of them
are true.

There was the principal who
kept her hot, tired teachers late
at an after-school meeting
while she read them a poem
of her own composing.
Twenty-six stanzas.
One for each letter of the alphabet.
On dental health.

There was the principal who
banished library books
from the classrooms
and forbade his teachers
to read to their children—
because he thought it interfered
with the basal scope-and-sequence chart.

There was the principal who . . .
but never mind.
This kind of talk
can pull me down pretty fast.

I will think instead of my current principal.
He is worth far more than rubies.
But not for a whole multipurpose room
full of rubies would I want his job.
It's sort of like being
a pastor or a president.
Everyone—*everyone*—
has an opinion about you.
And they're more than willing
to share it.
Stubborn superintendents.
Angry parents.
Frustrated teachers.
Life is a round of meetings
and paperwork,
and to top it all off,
misbehaving kids.

Yet he does the job with humor and kindness
when it's a wonder anyone can do it at all.

We don't pray for them enough,
do we, Father?
The principals, I mean.

Dear Lord,
preserve the good ones.
Improve (or remove!) the bad ones.
And let us all work together in harmony.

For the sake of our schools,
our kids.
Amen.

For the Librarian

Her title is:
Multimedia Learning Center Specialist.
But she has this thing about *books* . . .
So one day she rose up
and announced with crusty pride,
"I am a *li-brar-ian!*
And this—
this is a *library!*"
Then all the people said,
"Amen!"
So we made a new sign for her door.
And on the shelves,
the books were
grinning from cover to cover.

For the Consultants

Father,
I'm afraid there's a lot of friction here.
That's because
when you're a classroom teacher,
the world is divided
into two groups of people:
those who have to make a bunch of kids
shut up and sit down
and those who don't.

Consultants don't.

And furthermore,
they can go to the bathroom
anytime they want.
Most consultants, it's true,
used to be classroom teachers.
But the opinion from the trenches
is that they no longer wear the Green Beret.
Still,
it's not easy being a consultant,
working within a slow and clumsy system
where a child referred today
is lucky to get placed next year.
Father,
I'm afraid there's a lot of friction here.
We all need to be anointed
with the oil of your peace.

For the Team

Father, I'm afraid I often take these people for granted, but we wouldn't be able to have school without them. Lord, I want to thank you for the team.

Here is a person who greets all visitors to the school; who orients substitute teachers; who knows what callers want even when they're not sure themselves; who can understand what kindergartners are saying; who can read the most scribbled, cryptic notes from teachers; who watches over kids who are either too sick or too bad to go out for recess; who holds the place together and brings new meaning to the term *organized*. Lord, I want to thank you for the secretary!

When children get sick, they get scared. Even a mild stom-achache can seem like appendicitis to them. They need someone who responds with capable serenity, offers matter-of-fact sympa-thy. They also need someone who can spot a phony from clear down at the end of the hall. Lord, I want to thank you for the nurse!

Without going into details, sometimes something happens in my room that causes me to run gagging into the hall. That's when he calmly takes over. There are days when his job is not unlike that of a zookeeper in all its yuckiness. And even on the pleasantest days, classrooms need upkeep and repair. Lord, I want to thank you for the custodian!

Some people think kids are always bubbling over with eager questions about the universe. Not really; but there *is* one question that gets asked a lot: What's for lunch? For all their interest in food, it's heartbreaking to see the perfectly good food they throw away. It's even more distressing to watch them eat. A school cafeteria is not the pleasantest place in the world—most factories are quieter—but there are people who cheerfully care for school children in this special way. Lord, I want to thank you for the cafeteria workers!

Children are not the most alert of all your creatures. If some-body didn't stop them, they'd walk right out into the traffic. Somebody stops them. Lord, I want to thank you for the crossing guard!

Here is a person with nerves of steel, who takes on the awesome responsibility of getting a bunch of wired kids from there to here and back again. I can't imagine doing it. Lord, I want to thank you for the bus driver!

No, we couldn't have school without them. Lord, I want to thank you for the team!

Schooldaze

Oh, Lord . . . .

These tedious quarrels!
This petty pride!
Childish jealousies!
Choosing sides!
Not to mention
the snotty clique
going off
in a fit of pique!
School is wearisome at best.
(I had to get that off my chest.)
I came to you,
I'm glad I did,
but now let's talk
about the kids.

At the School Board Meeting

Lord,
let me feel you near me!
It's so hard to concentrate
in this burring, overheated room.
I'm here to represent my school.
And soon it will be my turn
to step out from the crowd
and address my well-reasoned plea
for smaller class sizes
to the school board.
They're sitting on the dais,

123

behind that staunch, impassive table,
and I have the strangest idea
that I won't be nearly big enough
to reach the microphone,
that my small voice will be swallowed
in the mechanical shrilling.
Nervously, I gulp the bitter, tepid coffee
and wait my turn to speak.

And suddenly I'm thinking
of the oddest things:

> the crisp, satisfying sound of scissors cutting into good
> construction paper;
>
> the yucky smell of lima beans wrapped in damp paper
> towels to germinate;
>
> the warm, trembly feel of the gerbil when I gently lift
> him out of his cage to say hello to everyone;
>
> the bright, orderly beauty of Cuisenaire rods in the mid-
> morning sunlight;
>
> the happy taste of popcorn on our Friday afternoons
> when soon it's going-home time and all's right with the
> world.

"Hey, you're on!"
The local newspaper reporter,
who covers education,
nudges me
and nods toward the microphone.

My turn.
My turn to somehow
make all these grown-ups see
that when class sizes are too large,
children have to wait too long
for their turn to hold the gerbil.
Lord, let me feel you near me!
I am a stranger far from home.

Elspeth Campbell Murphy is often asked about her first name. It is a Scottish form of Elizabeth, and is pronounced just as it's spelled, with the accent on the *El*. Elspeth was born in Hamilton, Scotland, near Glasgow. She spent her early years in Canada but has lived most of her life near Lake Michigan, first in Indiana and then in Illinois.

Elspeth has more than one hundred titles to her credit and sales exceeding six million copies worldwide. She is the author of the best-selling THREE COUSINS DETECTIVE CLUB® series and the new YOUNG COUSINS MYSTERIES®, a "prequel" series that takes the three cousins back a couple of years in story time. She is also well known for her best-selling series of psalm paraphrases for children, "David and I Talk to God," and her Gold Medallion book of prayers for young children, *Do You See Me, God?*

A graduate of Trinity College, Moody Bible Institute, and Oakland University with an M.A.T. in elementary education, Elspeth has taught in the elementary grades and written and edited curriculum. She now writes full time and lives with her husband, Michael, in Chicago. From her home-office window, Elspeth can see a school on one side and a zoo on the other. She says it's fun to go to sleep at night hearing the roar of the lions over the roar of the buses.